7 Steps To Grow Your Business With Events

Silvia Pellegrini

Copyright notice

Contents

Cultivating a Rare Bloom:
Planning for your Event

Events are not like flowers, which unfold naturally and beautifully because it is in their nature. If you want an event to come off well, you have to plan and prepare with care and attention to detail. You can afford to leave nothing to chance; your clients and their guests will expect smooth preparation, flawless execution, and a pleasurable experience. Fortunately, there are methodical steps you can take to ensure that your event will blossom into something spectacular.

Set Goals and Intentions First

Sit down with the stakeholders for the occasion and have a serious conversation about its purpose, their hopes and yours. Determine mutually agreeable goals. Have a list of questions at the ready, and answer them all to everyone's satisfaction before you move to the next step. I suggest these five basic event questions:

Five Basic Questions

1. *Why are you staging this event?* Is it to raise awareness of an issue? Celebrate someone's accomplishments? Generate funds for a worthy cause?

2. *What are the goals and desired outcomes?* What specific information would you like to convey to the public? Do you want to build a base of volunteers as well as raise cash? Will this retirement party set the bar for other employees' performance or expectations? Will this seminar establish your firm as the thought leader for your industry?

3. *Who are the desired participants for the event?* Who are the people you would like to attend? People with disposable income? Insurance professionals? Individuals who like to holiday in time-shared condos?

4. *How do you attract them?* What things does your target market care about? What do they enjoy doing?

5. *What will participants want from their attendance?* Really good cocktails? A smashing band? Knowledge that will give them a professional edge? A sense of emotional satisfaction?

You—and anyone else involved in the planning—need to be very clear on the answers to these questions before you proceed to next steps. And everyone involved should have a shared vision and commitment to a single plan...even if there is some disagreement about the details.

Choose a Theme

Once you have answered the five questions above, you will be ready to select a theme for the event. Theme is an important tool for event planning: it can attract potential participants, enhance marketing, and drive aesthetic choices. In short, the theme should allow you to organize all other elements around a central, unified idea. Your theme must suit the nature of the occasion. "A Night in Paris" may be perfect for a school dance, but will not suit a workshop on increasing SEO effectiveness for insurance provider websites. The theme determines the topics for a seminar or conference. It inspires the decorations for a wedding. It influences catering choices, dress expectations for participants, and so many other details. So choose the right one. It should be concise, clearly conceived and articulated, and appealing to your target market (as well as you and your clients).

If your event will require advance publicity, use the theme to create a short, punchy title. Be sure that and the organization and/or your clients' names are clearly visible on all related materials from the website to the postcards to the invitations.

Create the Calendar

Creating and maintaining a proper calendar is absolutely key to an event's success. Obviously, it begins with determining the date for the event itself, but don't allow yourself to stop there! Work backwards from that day, and determine milestones for every major objective that you must accomplish. Know when your marketing plan should be ready, and the date you plan to launch your publicity campaign. Know the dates that the invitations must be ordered, and when they must be sent. Include dates for contacting speakers or performers, for paying deposits and balances to caterers and other vendors. And of course, stick to the dates you determine. One must make adjustments as needed…delays do happen. But be disciplined about completing things on the due dates that you have established as far as it is in your own power.

Schedule and Activities

A well-planned event is one where each moment is carefully conceived and executed. Know what you want your guests/participants to think, feel, do, and experience from the moment they arrive at your doors to the moment they return to their homes. If you will include activities—from paper presentations or demonstrations to games—play attention to the scheduling. Make sure that the activities resonate with your theme, and that their titles reflect the title for the overall event.

Keep your guests engaged and involved. If your event has an educational character, make sure that all the elements are on message, and that the format is designed to help participants acquire the knowledge fully. If your primary goal is simply to offer people a pleasant evening in one another's company, consider their tastes and desires in music, food, and entertainment. Give people time to rest— don't send them scrambling frenetically from one lecture to the next.

Keep your participants informed at every step. Make sure they have materials with the event schedule, or that the time table is clearly posted where everyone can see it. Provide them with information that explains clearly what they will see, hear, and experience. Small surprises during the event are acceptable—little treats, unexpected guests, and humorous encounters. But don't keep them guessing about what content they might encounter, or how you expect them to participate and respond. A big part of managing their expectations is giving guests plenty of information, and telling them what your own intentions and expectations are for the event.

Event Materials

A printed schedule, such as I mentioned above, is only one type of event-related material. Plan yours well and plan them in advance. Ask yourself what guests will need, or what they will enjoy. And, of course, what your budget may allow. This may include programs or timetables. It might include name badges, workbooks and textbooks. You may wish to offer small gifts, promotional items, and souvenirs

—these can range from t-shirts to pens to coffee mugs and key rings, or small bags of sweets and bottled water.

As with all things, any materials that you offer your guests should fit in with your theme. If possible, they should be tagged with the title of the event and/or with the name and logo of your clients' and their organizations.

Like flowers, events can be beautiful things. They give people pleasure, make life easier and more satisfying. Cultivate yours properly from the start.

How much?
Building and Sticking to an Event Budget

Ask any event planner for their top questions when meeting potential clients; you might get a variety of answers, but I can guarantee almost all of them would include "How much do you have to spend?" It doesn't matter whether it is a simple affair or a lavish one; you need a clear picture of the budget—what you've got and how you are going to use it—for things to come off well.

I think the process of budgeting can be a bit overwhelming for people, though. How do you even know where to start? That's where a professional event planner can be a significant help, in organizing the expenses and helping clients understand how to get the most out of their available funds. I think it helps to start by determining all of the possible sources of expense at the outset.

<u>20 Questions to Determine Expenses</u>

- Who will attend?
- Will you need to hire a venue?
- Will parking be made available?
- Will refreshments be offered? If so, what kind and how often (tea, full meals?)
- Will entertainment be provided? What kind?
- Will there be any activities, games, or excursions?

- Will the event be documented (video, photography, press coverage, etc.)?
- Will travel be necessary for participants? Who will bear the cost?
- Will lodging be necessary for participants? Who will bear the cost?
- Will transport be necessary to/from the venue?
- Should anyone be paid for their participation (speakers, special guests)?
- Will there be printed materials (invitations, programs, stationery, name badges, etc.)?
- Will there be a need to advertise/market the event?
- Will any permits be required for the event?
- Will there be a need for insurance or medical care?
- Will there be a need for security?
- Will there be a need for staff (waiters, bartenders, translators, A/V technicians, etc.)?
- Do you wish to decorate the space?
- Will any equipment be needed (a sound system, tables and chairs)?
- Will you provide gifts or mementos to any participants?

Asking these questions and making a printed list of the answers is an excellent idea, especially if someone has vague expectations of cost and grand schemes for what they want. Haven't we all met a bride with dreams of live swans floating about in the fountains?

Expense	Estimated Cost	Actual Cost
Venue Hire		
Rentals (table/chairs)		
Presenter/Entertainer		
Audio/Visual Equipment hire		
Advertising/Promotion		
Stationary/Printing/Photocopy		
Postage/Telephone		
Speaker		
Food/Catering		
Decorations		
Transportation/Travel		
Security/Technician		
Accommodation		
Medical fees/Insurance		
Activities		
Contingency funds		
Total expenses:		

Once you have determined all of the possible places you *could* spend money, it makes sense to go back through your list and decide where you *should* spend money, especially if there is a limit to the available funds (and there almost always is). Start by listing everything you might wish to have for the event.

Do the research on the costs to purchase, hire, or lease each one. When the final numbers are there on the paper, it should help create realistic expectations; then you may go back and start make choices based on what the event needs and what it can do without.

Knowing how much to spend is essential, of course. But so is a clear sense of where the money comes from. For certain social events— weddings and birthday parties, for example—funds usually come directly from the event organizers. The bride and groom save up, the family chips in, and so on. For professional events like workshops, trade shows, and society meetings, funds might come from the organizers, or from sponsors, or from participant fees.

Once you have your list of responses to the 20 questions, consult this list of potential funding sources. Determine which are most appropriate for your event, and calculate how much each will provide.

- Personal/company funds
- Family/friend contributions
- Sponsorships (local businesses, government offices, clubs)
- Partnerships (local businesses, government offices, clubs)
- Participant fees

- Ticket sales
- Merchandise sales (souvenirs, shirts, books, etc.)
- Exhibition space

Once you have determined where the money might come from, do the follow up to make sure it will actually be there when you need it. For example, if a party is to be paid for with contributions from a group of extended family, make sure there is a firm commitment from each person. See to it that the cheques are written. If you intend to sell advertisements in the program or booth space in an exhibition hall, first conduct a survey to see if anyone has interest in purchasing those options. Based on the number of "yes" responses, calculate the quantity that you actually believe will sell. Set early deadlines for fees so you can adjust your budget if those sales come in under target. The same is true for ticket sales and registration fees.

In any case, the final budget should be determined by how much can be raised for expenses, not how much you wish to spend (except, perhaps, if you are Bill Gates or Rupert Murdoch. Then you can do what you like). When you have hard figures for the available cash, make firm decisions on where best to spend it and stick to them. Write Everything Down.

Creating spreadsheets can be a chore, and if you don't relish making your own from scratch, there are many free templates available online.

Revenue	Expected Revenue	Actual Revenue
Ticket sales/Participant fees		
Merchandise sale/ Food sales		
Vendor fees/ Exhibition space		
Event sponsorship		
Partnership		
Donations		
Other		
Total Revenue:		

As you plan your event, look for opportunities to cut costs—can you rent an item instead of buying it? Can you borrow it instead of renting? Can a less expensive substitute be found (potted plants instead of fresh flowers)? If potential sponsors are unwilling to donate cash, would they be willing to make in kind donations instead —say trays of biscuits or program printing in exchange for an advertising display somewhere in the event space? Can you negotiate a discount from a vendor if you agree to use their business for several of your budget items, or for more than one event? While you should consider your budget "fixed" in the sense that you should avoid spending more than you have, try to keep an eye out for ways to save cost during the whole process. If you do, then you might be able to free up some funds for something you wanted at the outset but felt was out of reach. The bride might get her swans after all!

Meet Your Match: Attracting the Right Attendees to your Corporate Event

A successful professional seminar or business workshop is the result of careful planning and a lot of hard work. No event planner will deny this fact. But success is also determined by the people who attend, and that is a factor of <u>who you invite</u>—and that isn't only true for presenters, but for participants, as well.

A successful event depends on inviting the right attendees; that is absolutely central to getting solid attendance numbers. It is also important for your business or organization as a whole. The people you want to be there are the ones who will eagerly purchase your products or services, the ones who want to learn what you have to teach, and who will go out and spread the word about the fabulous experience they had with you.

Where should you begin? With your current customers, of course. These are the people who know you and what you can provide. They should receive first word about a new event. They are pre-disposed to buy from you, especially if you reward their loyalty with the promise of discounted admission or another special benefit. This could be anything from complimentary texts/materials to personal interaction with the celebrity keynote speaker. When you make first marketing contact about the event, make sure to highlight what will be new, unique, or special about this experience. While your current customers may love the experiences they have already had with you, and this may be enough to draw them back, remember that this is like any other relationship. You don't want it to become stale. Surprise them, engage them, and you will keep them coming back again and again.

And encourage those customers to bring a friend. Perhaps they have already done some word-of-mouth advertising for you. Seminars and workshops are a perfect opportunity to encourage that activity. Everyone likes company when they attend an event, and if they are excited about your product or service they will be keen to share it with their social and professional circles. Offer an enticement for referring a friend: a small discount on their own fees, a prize or gift, perhaps even free admission for themselves if they can sign up x number of attendees.

It is also important to activate your social and professional networks. Your business contacts, friends and family should be kept in the loop for all of your upcoming events. Tell them—concisely but clearly—who stands to benefit from attending (this is your target market, so you should already have complete data), and make sure they have access to all of the relevant marketing materials, especially electronic versions that can easily be shared. If anyone in these circles is in your key demographic, invite them to attend as your guest. Offer a special price or discount for their own friends, should they wish bring a group. If you employ professional business introducers, make sure they are among the first to receive the information about your event. Give them a clear description of your target market—in writing! —that includes a careful, complete summary of the value that you will provide to attendees. Also, remember this: when your personal and professional contacts <u>do</u> come through in spreading the word, reward them! Say thank you to everyone who helps you, preferably in a tangible way, with a small gift of some kind.

As you interact with the media, go to the right outlets. Radio, television, publications and social media can all be powerful tools for getting the message out, but only if you choose the right ones. Which ones do your target demographic read, watch and follow? Those are the ones to approach for press releases, advertisements, editorials and the like. If you meet up with any special "influencers", for example an individual who operates a popular blog or Twitter feed, invite them to attend as your guest. If appropriate, offer a commission on any attendance fees you take in from their networks. (Warning! Exercise caution and judgment when making this offer. In some circles it is perfectly acceptable, but for others it is a serious breach of etiquette.)

And finally, partner with organizations. Are there professional societies that exist for the discipline you intend to cover? Are there interest groups associated with the topic? Or charitable and nonprofit organizations whose members need the expertise you can offer? Contact any such groups operating in the area where your workshop or seminar will be held. Research any local groups that may be in reasonable travel distance. Notify them with the details of your event; they will have their own social networks and lists of members and can pass that information along. If appropriate, offer to recognize attendees from the organizations that partner with you, or tailor content to meet their needs.

The people that you want to see filling the hall at your event (and who want to meet you!) are accessible in many ways. Start with your networks, and remember that each person in those networks has networks of their own. Be clear about what you have to offer, and exactly whom the event is for. Recognize and appreciate any efforts that are made on your behalf. These are the keys to attracting your ideal attendees.

The Date Won't Wait:
The Secret to Scheduling a Successful Event

Every bride gets accustomed to hearing "Have you set a date yet?" from all sides. But picking the perfect day for that "special day" isn't just important for weddings. Every event planner should have the ability to offer sound counsel in the matter of choosing a date for public events and special occasions.

And setting a date is not simply a matter of personal preference for the organizers! There are a number of important considerations that must be weighed. Of course, some of the variables will have a different weight depending upon whether the event is a private affair like a birthday party or christening, or a public/professional gathering such as a political rally or conference. It will always be important to check the schedules of the desired participants, however. How one does this will also differ according to the nature of the affair.

Personal vs. Public Affairs

For a private occasion, the most important considerations are the availability of the "key participants." You can't have a wedding without a bride and groom, or a birthday party without the birthday boy/girl. The first step is to consult their wishes about the date for the event. After that, you can begin coordinating with the people with whom they wish to share the celebration.

For a public event, you can't really go about asking a whole demographic to check their calendars. But you can check existing public events calendars—often maintained by local authorities or chambers of commerce—to see what civic and social events are already on the books. You must also consider statistically how people choose to spend their time on major holidays, weekends, and public occasions. If the local or regional newspapers or alternate press publish an events calendar, examine it to see if major sport or entertainment events are upcoming.

Three Steps to Setting the Date

In any case, there are three basic steps for setting an event date: Set the Season, Select the Day, and Fix the Time.

Setting the Season

First is to settle on the right time of year for your event. The main idea is to choose a season that with benefits you can use to your advantage while avoiding major conflicts. Christmas time might be perfect for a banquet to benefit the homeless, because people tend to feel more generosity at the holidays. But it is a terrible time to schedule a professional seminar, because they want to spend time with their families.

Especially if your desired participants are in a specific subculture, profession, community or group, know their annual schedules. For example, know when accountants tend to have their busy season. Know when students have their final exams. Know the important holy days for the major religions.

DO

- Choose a season that enhances the mood/atmosphere you want the event to cultivate.
- Choose the season that best suits your venue (no outdoor receptions in the hottest month).
- Make sure to check weather and climate tendencies for each month in your location.
- Ask venues when they tend to have fewer bookings.
- Check the calendar for major celebrations (holidays, parades, memorials) in that season.

DON'T

- Schedule during a season when people will feel that it conflicts with their other responsibilities.
- Schedule when airfares and hotels rates tend to be high.
- Schedule close to times of major financial expense (Christmas, tax day, etc.).

Select the Day

Once you have chosen the perfect season, you can set about selecting a day. This is the time to begin consulting calendars. If you are planning a private event, start sending out e-mails or making phone calls to everyone on the prospective guest list. If you are planning a public event, consult the community calendar, contact anyone on your list of speakers/presenters/special guests, and do some basic research on the habits of your target group. If a professional association or club will be involved, ask them for their official calendar and for an informal list of their typical activities during a given month. Summer months and major holiday periods tend to be busier, so consider whether it is possible to avoid those times.

The day of the week you choose should fit the nature of the occasion. Social events are usually better attended on weekends; work or professional events should take place during the workweek. Your attendance will be higher if your potential guests feel it will not disrupt their typical schedule.

Did you know that a professional study was conducted a few years ago to help determine the best days to schedule events where fees and funding are involved? Howard Shenson, the researcher, discovered the following:

WHEN THE PARTICIPANT PAYS THEIR OWN FEES, THEIR PREFERENCES, IN ORDER, ARE:

January, September, October, March, April, June, November, February, May, July, December, August

FOR DAYS OF THE WEEK:

Wednesday, Thursday, Tuesday, Friday, Saturday, Monday, Sunday

WHEN SOMEONE ELSE PAYS THE BILL, THEY PREFER:

March, October, April, September, November, January, February, June, May, July, August, December

FOR DAYS OF THE WEEK:

Saturday, Sunday, Thursday, Wednesday, Tuesday, Friday, Monday

If participants will be traveling, something they might do for a major personal occasion like a golden anniversary or for a professional event like a trade show, take into account that travel adds an additional scheduling burden for their lives. Plan social events for times when whole families can attend; plan professional events for times that tend to be "slow" or "quiet" within the industry.

— Check the community calendar for events that might compete with yours—sport, parades, elections, even popular television shows can affect your numbers.

— Check for religious and civic occasions that might cause conflict.

— Select up to 3 potential dates for your event.

— Research your target audience's habits—do they attend church? Do most have children?

— Ask participants and stakeholders for their availability well in advance.

— Consider scheduling a day before or after another major event if that will increase your numbers (scheduling your band to play the day before a major music festival opens).

DON'T

— Schedule on a day when participants must choose between another attractive event and yours.

— Schedule too close to a major social, professional, or religious obligation.

Fix the Time

The same essential rules that apply for setting a date are also applicable for choosing the time of day. Social events should occur during hours when your desired guests are free from their professional or educational obligations. Professional events should not take time away from leisure unless absolutely necessary.

Try to imagine practical concerns of participants. Are they parents? Then they might need to return home early in the evening. Do they have to travel a long way? Then allow them time for that commute for in choosing arrival and departure times.

DO

- Consider the typical schedule of your target demographic.
- Take into account the logistics of travel, transport, parking, etc.
- Schedule a sufficient block of time to include all planned activities.
- Consider the venue's capabilities at different times of day.
- Allow some break between activities for participants to refresh themselves.

DON'T

- Schedule starting or ending times at a very late (or very early) hour, if you can avoid it.
- Allow blocks of unscheduled time, or long gaps between activities.
- Overlap starting or ending times with other important events.

A solid turn out for your event will depend both on whether the invited participants *want* to attend and whether they are *able* to attend. The former is a matter of marketing—making the occasion sound so amazing, so valuable that they would hate to be left out. But the latter is just as important. Guests count on you to create a schedule that maximizes their experience and minimize their inconvenience.

Location Makes Occasion:

Choosing the Right Venue for the Event

Real estate agents and entrepreneurs rave about the importance of "location, location, location." Smart event planners know that venue can make all the difference to a well-planned occasion, too. Choosing a suitable venue makes a difference for the tone of the event, the quality of the guests' experience, and ultimately, your clients' satisfaction. So do it mindfully.

Do the Numbers

How many guests will be invited? How many will actually attend? The venue must be just the right size. A too-small auditorium makes for an uncomfortable, ill-tempered crowd, especially if they cannot find a place to sit down or rest a drink. A too-large space gives the impression of low attendance (and often falsely so). You and your clients may make either decision first—how many people to invite, or where to hold the party—but the two must always be in proportion. If the organizers hope that 100,000 fans will attend the concert, pick a *very* big field. If the bride simply must have that gorgeous chapel, then she will have to make some tough decisions about who will be snubbed. Take the guesswork out by doing your homework on the potential size of the crowd before you fix on a location.

And Those Numbers, Too

Of course budget is also a key concern! Before you begin investigating possibilities, you should have a sound idea of how much is allowed for venue costs. And be sure when you speak to the management to inquire about *all* fees associated with their space. One place may allow guests to bring their own refreshments; another may charge a corking fee or insist on their own concessions sales. If there will be costs above and beyond the simple use of the space, you will want to know that early on, so inquire up front. Also, ask if your participants will encounter fees—parking, food, ticket surcharges—so that you can advise them early.

As a professional, you may be able to develop relationships with the management of certain places and receive consideration or discount for repeat business. You also may be able to negotiate a lower price for booking at a less busy season or time of day. You can propose different terms in exchange for using the same venue/company on multiple occasions (this works very well for conferences, especially with hotel chains). There are a number of techniques you can use to try and reduce the costs of venue hire. But in the end, it will be up to you to be the voice of reason about expense. Do it gently and kindly, but firmly—keep co-organizers and clients within their fixed budget for the space.

A Sense of Occasion for the Occasion

A more formal or serious affair should have different surroundings than a festival or family reunion. Organizers should do more than scan the brochures or surf the websites; visit the candidates—at least the top 3 picks—to confirm that they have the right *feel* for the event. Does the décor suit your theme, or clash with it? Will great quantities of decorations be necessary to dress the space appropriately for the highflying keynote speaker and celebrity guests you have invited? Will the elderly couple feel uncomfortable in a room with gilt, mirrors, and ostentatious trimmings worthy of Versailles?

If the event will have a very formal tone, then by all means, prioritize a venue with attractive appointments and well-conceived spaces. But take care that the design also matches the social and cultural tone of the occasion. The annual meeting for a national company or diplomatic mission ought to occur in a beautiful space, but not in one that is floridly decorated with vivid prints or rococo angels. If the religious organization hosting the charity ball is very conservative, take care that those marble nudes can be covered or moved before you put down a deposit. Fundraising events should take care to avoid the impression that they do not really *need* the money they are raising.

Matters of Taste

The clients' and guests' tastes should also be considered when evaluating the available properties. If the family says they like a modern look, then it is best not to push for the Victorian mansion. Ask the stakeholders for the event about both the tone and their tastes. How formal or informal do they wish things to be? What kinds of design do they like? Is there a particular period or fashion that they adore or abhor? Are there specific colours that should be included or avoided?

What about the guests or participants? Do they tend to belong to a particular social group, economic class, or political/cultural event? Then they will also have opinions about the surroundings, and their experience of the event may be influenced by whether they find the venue aesthetically pleasing.

Let the Function Lead Form

As you inspect potential locations, keep in mind the activities that are likely to occur at the event and make wise choices. It is a good idea to make a list of possible activities before you start calling.

Here are two possible scenarios:

Laura and Ned's Wedding	InterCorp Sales Workshop
Ceremony with 10 attendants	200 participants
Bar & hors d'oeuvres	Large lecture
Full service dinner	Break out sessions in groups of 10
Dancing	Team-building exercise with footballs
Live band	Tea break (2)

As you consider possible locations for the event, having a list of likely/scheduled activities will allow you to consider whether there is an appropriate amount room for everything you have planned, and whether the available space can be configured to suit your needs.

Pay attention to the condition of each facility when you visit. There are many places that look stunning on first glance, but turn out to have ancient fixtures and fossilised plumbing. Inspect the electrics and lighting, the toilets, the carpets—any place your guests might wander. Look for signs of wear or bad repair. If you see anything that makes you uncomfortable or seems cause for alarm, imagine how your guests might respond and consider looking elsewhere. Be VERY careful with management promises to fix anything or complete renovations before your chosen date.

At the same time, remember to inquire about the management's rules and restrictions for the use of their property. Understand, they have an active investment in the care of their facilities, and in their own financial well being. So ask for, and read, the literature on their policies. Do they prohibit smoking? Are the portraits on the wall sacrosanct, or can they be covered? Are you responsible for your own clean up? Can you throw rice or birdseed? When in doubt, ask. No one likes to be confronted by an angry caretaker in the middle of the evening's proceedings.

Anticipate Participant Needs

This should never be an afterthought. Even if the venue is a sparkling gem, guests will remember if parking was a nightmare or the toilets backed up in the first hour. So make choices with their comfort and convenience in mind. Make sure that parking and transportation to/from the event is manageable. If participants will be coming from out of town, or long hours will be expected, that affordable lodging and food can be found nearby. Make sure that adequate toilet and rest facilities are available (another reason to carefully calculate your attendance numbers). If families with small children will be present, remember that they will need surfaces for nappy-changing (unless you want them doing this out in the open). Consider the possibility that some participants may need accommodation for mobility limitations or other physical issues, particularly if you expect an older crowd.

It is a lot to consider! Your ideal venue is one that combines comfort, pleasant surroundings, and a reasonable fee. It can be a challenge. But in the end, remember that everything you handle at the start is one more thing that will not cause headaches on the big day.

Get the Message:

Marketing for Your Event

It is a universally acknowledged truth that if you want people to show up for an event, you have to inform them about it. This is a relatively simple matter for private occasions like weddings and birthday parties—you and your clients simply decide who should be present, create an attractive invitation, and send it out via post or the web. For public events, from political fundraisers to paid seminars to civic celebrations, things get a bit more complicated. And that is why a competent event planner needs to know a thing or two about marketing.

There are a number of techniques that anyone can use to get the word out in advance of an event. But before you begin, you need to be certain that you understand the area and the people where you plan to broadcast your message. Read up on the advertising techniques that have proven success in the local market. Talk to members of the industry, clubs, or associations based in the area and ask them what works and which methods are considered acceptable and which are rude or disallowed. Familiarise yourself with the regional media, including newspapers and magazines, television, and radio. Keep a running list of the available outlets and the potential marketing tools at your disposal for the specific market. This is important whether you are based in a single city, or if you are responsible for planning and promoting events internationally. It is absolutely essential that you do this research if you plan to promote an occasion in unfamiliar, or multiple, locations. What works well for one large city may utterly fail in the village fifty miles away.

You should also have a strong sense of how many people you would like to attend (and if there are limits to the number you can manage with regard to food, space, accommodation, and the like). Know the number of attendees that you need to turn a profit, or make a strong statement, or make your clients happy.

When you know the market and have set goals for attendance, your next step involves creating two things: a message, and a marketing plan.

The message should come first. It is your job to make the occasion sound so compelling that people simply can't bear the thought of missing it! After all, the success of your event is half determined by the size of the turnout (and the other half, of course, is whether your participants are pleased with the experience you offer them). You need a clear picture of your target market—who is it you want to attend your event? —and you need to know what to say to get their attention. Having your marketing message right will help you draw people to the event, and will invite media coverage and word-of-mouth to increase your reach. Create a short description that sells the event, preferably paired with an attractive visual presentation, and <u>be</u> <u>consistent</u> in using that material for every promotional outlet. If you struggle with messaging, or have little experience, it is probably worthwhile to hire a marketing professional who can help you describe your event in a way that will make the public notice and get excited. If budget is a concern, you can still handle the advertising and distribution on your own, but get an expert to help you create the materials.

Once the message and materials are ready, formalise and execute your marketing plan by deciding which channels you will use to distribute information about the event, and how frequently this should be done. Aim to use a mix of channels; different groups of potential attendees pay attention to different media outlets. Some read newspapers, others prefer television, and still others tend to notice posters at their favourite coffee house. The perfect marketing plan is one that maximizes your reach and keeps expense to a minimum. Some of the best and/or most common outlets include:

E-mail

If you have, or can get, a contact list for your target market, e-mail promotion is a terrific way to distribute your message. The cost is very low (free if you already have a contact list), and if your invitation sparks interest, many people will forward your messages to their own social networks—instant scalability. If you have contacts with their own e-mail lists, speak with them about the possibility of sending your invitation out. If yours is a paid event, you can offer them a share of revenues raised from their network. An e-mail management service like Constant Contact or Emma is a godsend if you plan on sending mass messages, or send frequent updates. Send messages often enough to be memorable, but not so often as to be a nuisance. Start with an initial message 3-4 months out; follow up monthly until the month of your event. Then send out weekly updates, and one per day for 2-3 days beforehand. Then send a follow up immediately after, thanking attendees and highlighting the most successful aspects.

Direct Mail/Print

This can include posters, handbills, and flyers—any printed-paper item that you might send out via post or display in a public place. There was a time when direct mail advertising offered a strong return on investment for event promotion. But the explosions of web-based communication and increased prices for both postage and print services have lessened its effect. There may still be an advantage to printing flyers or posters, which you can then hand out or mail to businesses/organizations with a request to display them in a visible area.

Media Advertising

If you have a sufficient budget and wish to communicate with a broad public, then newspapers, magazines, radio, and television stations will still sell advertising. These methods tend to be expensive; you must pay for the advertisement or spot to be created —which means hiring a graphic designer, writer, and possibly actors —and for the actual time/space for the finished product. If you use media advertising, choose your outlets wisely. For example, a trade publication may be a better choice than a daily newspaper for your target market. Do your research on the demographic that the media outlet reaches before you approach them to purchase advertising. Don't waste time with outlets that your target market ignores.

Media Coverage

Of course, you can always aim for *free* coverage from media outlets by encouraging journalistic coverage of your event. Again, message is key. Television and radio stations, magazines and newspapers get hundreds of promotional notices per year. Send press releases with the most compelling description you can create, be polite and persistent in inviting them to interview you or your clients, and don't be disappointed if someone says "No thanks."

Once your marketing plan is in place, execute it with discipline and stick to it. Only change or cut strategies if you have clear evidence that they do not work. No matter what channels you choose for your advertising, make sure that the public has multiple ways of contacting you for information. Create a website (and keep it updated!). Have an e-mail address and phone number where they can call you. Publicize very clear directions to the event location. If your target market is web 2.0 savvy, utilize Facebook, Twitter, YouTube and LinkedIn.

If your message and your marketing plan are sound, you will stand a much better chance of staging a successful, well attended event. It all comes down to communication: make sure yours is clear, compelling, and consistent.

When You Speak of Me, Speak Kindly:

The Secrets of Great Client Testimonials

Winning a potential customer's trust can be a challenge. Why shouldn't it be? You are a perfect stranger, and everyone's mother taught them never to talk to strangers. Event planning is an industry with certain reputation management problems, thanks to that small, but unsavoury body of unscrupulous vendors who promise big and deliver small. Little wonder, then, that our clients have trust issues. But you know whom customers do trust? Other customers.

If you have a contingent of happy former customers who were thrilled with the event you put together for them, then you can harness all of that love to build credibility. Yes, you have confidence that their word-of-mouth references will send friends and family to your door. But you can also use their enthusiasm to gain the confidence of perfect strangers. Testimonials can be among your most powerful tools for winning new clients, if you manage them properly.

How is this done? First, it is necessary to recognise the importance of peer-to-peer information sharing in the Internet age. There is a reason that reputation management is a booming branch of the consulting industry. (With that in mind, a brief word of advice:

always let your clients know how important their thoughts and feedbacks are to you. Give them proof that you take their responses to heart.)

You have probably taken advantage of online reviews yourself, reading consumer ratings of products and services before making a purchasing decision...probably even when deciding where to go out for cocktails on the weekend. The same principle applies with client testimonials posted to your own website and social media profiles— with the added benefit that you have more direct control over these than you would a rating on a public consumer site.

A perfect client testimonial is brief, specific, and articulate. It should not exceed 150 words; it should contain no spelling or grievous grammatical errors. It speaks of the professional in warm and enthusiastic tones, but without hyperbole or becoming overly effusive....no one should suspect that it was written by your Mum. The right testimonial creates a positive picture of you as a skilled expert with specific abilities.

Here are five simple guidelines to help you get the most out of your testimonials:

1. *Be prepared to collect them at the event or soon after*. People can speak in the most compelling detail when their memories are fresh. You can pass out a comment form at the end of the seminar. You can hand pick a few individuals and

present them with a response card. If you are coordinating an event with a client you know well, you can ask permission to video short clips or take pictures of pre-selected individuals. You might even ask them to help you select those persons.

If circumstances prevent you from connecting with respondents at the event, then give them an opportunity to follow up soon after. Slip a pre-paid postcard in the seminar materials. Send a follow up e-mail summarizing the highlights of the occasion and inviting attendees to reply and share their thoughts. Invite them to engage with your social media profiles and post comments. You can also set up a survey online using a service like SurveyMonkey.com. Consider offering a small 'thank you' for their time: a discount for future event registration, the chance to win a prize or another small give-away like an informative white paper.

2. *Have prompts at the ready.* This is a situation where it is perfectly acceptable to lead the witness. Have a handful of very carefully crafted questions that guide the respondent to describe something specific. What was their favorite part of the event? Was there a problem or difficulty that they felt you handled especially well? What lasting information or

impression will they take with them? What do they think they will remember in a year's time? How did you (or the event) help them? How did it meet or exceed their expectations?

3. *Be prepared to take advantage of a compliment.* If someone stops you to say how impressed they are, ask them to take a moment and provide a tutorial. People like to feel that their opinions are valuable.

4. *Make good use of respondents' time.* If you hold someone more than 5-7 minutes while you fiddle with a camera's focus, muck about with a microphone, or ask endless questions, you will cause them to lose patience. And when they lose patience, you lose their goodwill. The quality of their testimonial will suffer. So be quick and efficient, thank them enthusiastically for their time, and get them on their way.

5. *Get their permission. In writing. No exceptions.* If you want to use someone's words—and especially if you want to include their name and image—getting their written permission is absolutely essential. Carry permission forms with you if you plan to collect video and/or audio on the fly. Include a clause on printed or online surveys advising respondents that their words may be used for marketing purposes, and include a box they can tick if they want to opt-out. (Most won't, but

everyone likes to be asked for their permission.) Post content only from those respondents who have agreed that you may use their words and likeness. As a courtesy, you might let them know when you are about to publish their testimonial and where it will appear.

Once you've got these written professions of love and respect, select the clearest and most compelling. These can be lightly edited—trimmed down, or smoothing away slight infelicities of language. Be careful never to change someone's meaning or alter the text too far from its original state. If necessary, hire a professional editor and wordsmith to help you edit, proofread and curate them. Once they are up on your website and profiles, make sure that a visitor can easily locate them. It just may be the one occasion when posting those love letters can help you win new friends!

Appendix 1- 6 Months Countdowns to your Event

Event planners are highly organized people. If you are in charge of organizing an event, this checklist will help you ensure all of the important details are covered. Use this checklist to cover all of your bases as the day approaches.

6 months:

- What are the goals, the purpose and the desired outcome of this event?

- Who is the target audience?

- When is an ideal time to hold the event?

- Who would the keynote speakers be and how many would be required?

- What is the estimated allocated budget?

- Where are the desired locations to hold the event?

- Who will be in charge of organizing various tasks?

5 months:
Social Calendar

- Are they any major events on at this time of year?

- Are there any midterms or public holidays near the event date?

Keynote Speakers

— Make a list of desired keynote speakers and contact them to check availability

— Do these speakers charge a fee?

— Will they require overnight accommodation?

— Will they require travel expenses?

— What topic do you require them to cover?

— How long do you want their speech to be?

— Do they require Internet access?

— Do they need a projector and a white screen?

— How many power points will they require?

— Will they have any other representatives with them?

Location

— Compile a list of preferred locations contacting them for pricing and availability

— Visit each location to make sure venue is suitable

— Do they have ample/free/ paying parking?

— What menus are available? Can they be mixed and matched?

— What are the accommodation costs?

- What equipment can they provide? Projectors, screens etc

- Will the room hold the required amount of tables and stands?

4 months:

- Finalize the decision on location, taking into account price and equipment available

- The keynote speakers available and all costs associated with them

- A list of equipment that may need to be hired externally and the costs associated with them

- Decision on menus and refreshments and price

- A final decision on the amount of attendees required and preferred method of contact

- Structure a loose timetable of the event itself

- A decision on the theme for all associated materials, invitations, brochures, leaflets and backdrops

- Gather a list of preferred design agencies along with quotes

- Define the estimated budget in more detail

3 months:

- Contact selected design agency with design brief and confirm cost

- Creative work should commence

- Confirm booking with hotel

- Confirm in writing a list of equipment being provided by hotel

- Confirm times on room availability

- Book any external equipment that maybe needed

- Draw up a structured timetable of the event day

- Contact all keynote speakers and confirm time and place

- Notify each speaker as to the time they'll be speaking and how long for

- Draw up a streamlined database of all potential attendees

- If inviting the public look at methods of applying for invitations and decide on a closing date for applications

- First drafts of creative material should be proofed after four weeks of creative

2 months:

- Creative material should be near completion

- Final invitation list should be drawn up

- Confirm lead times for creative material to be printed

- Solidify actual budget costs

- If inviting the public an advertisement in the local paper is advisable at least 6 weeks prior to event day

- All creative material should be printed approximately 5 weeks before event date

- Organise an anonymous questionnaire for attendees, this information will be useful for future events and for general feedback.

1 month:

<u>4 weeks</u>

- Send out invitations with an RSVP date

- Contact keynote speakers to confirm attendance

- Contact hotel to confirm booking

- Contact external equipment suppliers to confirm booking

<u>3 weeks</u>

- Print a program for the event for each guest

- Organise name tags for keynote speakers

- Have a database to record RSVP list

- Organise event packs for guests, such as pens, calendars, stress balls…

- Check that budgetary requirements are on target

<u>2 weeks</u>

- Ask for a copy of all the keynote speakers speeches

- Send each keynote speaker a copy of the event program and timetable

- Check that the attendance list is growing

- Submit a press release to the local newspaper

- Insert an advertisement in the local newspaper

- Distribution of leaflets

- Confirm accommodation bookings with hotel

- Contact hotel to confirm what time the room will be available for set-up

- Contact external equipment suppliers to notify them of room availability including time to run through the operating of the equipment

1 week

- Confirm final guest list allowing for last minute changes

- Confirm with hotel food and refreshment requirements

- Confirm with keynote speakers that they are satisfied with the event timetable

- Send a press release to local newspaper

- Insert an advertisement into the local newspaper

- Draw up a list of tasks to be completed on the day.

- 3-4 days prior to event print out final attendee list for registration

- Print off feedback questionnaires to give out at the end of the event

On the Day:

- Meet with daytime duty manager

- Check room has been cleaned

- Check that all equipment being provided by the hotel is in good working order

- Have all printed material and guest packs delivered by early afternoon make sure there is a sufficient supply its better to have too much as to too little

- Have a list of external equipment suppliers names and mobile numbers

- Ensure all equipment has been delivered setup and fully checked through by early afternoon

- Confirm time with suppliers for the return of the equipment, if not till the following day allocate somebody to look after the equipment when the event is over

- Have the list on keynote speakers with mobile numbers ready to hand

- Ensure that keynote speakers arrive at least an hour and a half before event launch, this is to ensure they are happy with the room set-up

- All display stands are set up

- Set up meet and greet area have name tags for keynote speakers and local business people displayed

- On meet and greet table have the registration list in alphabetical order ready for guests arrival

- Have questionnaires available for everyone to fill in also supply pens

- Ensure that all Internet and power points are working and useable

- Ensure podium, microphone and projector is working

- Confirm with hotel that tea and coffee will be served on arrival

- Confirm time for food service if speeches overrun contact duty manager and express a delay

- Meet with evening duty manager and run through a list of requirements

- Have a list of local press contacts with mobile numbers, contact them late afternoon to ensure their arrival

- Adequate seating is available make sure there are extra seats to hand in the event extra guests should arrive

After the Event

- Insure that all equipment has been returned to the supplier

- Request a preliminary invoice from hotel before leaving and check list that all services were supplied before actual invoice arrives

- Analyze feedback questionnaires and enter information into a database

- Compile a database of attendees to include name, phone number email

- Compile a report on verbal feedback received from attendees

- Ring local press and thank them for turning up

- Send out all thank you letters to all attendees/to the keynote speakers

- Pay all suppliers

- Finalize budget and actual costs of the event evening.

Glossary

Attendees: A group of people attending an event, for a range of purposes, from watching the event take place, to actively participating in some or all of the event's activities.

Break-even: The point at which an event's costs equal the revenue received for it.

Capacity: The maximum number of people who can be accommodated at a venue.

Client: The person or organization purchasing or specifying an event.

Conference: A meeting whose purpose is the interchange of ideas.

Corporate hospitality: Involves inviting groups or people, usually clients of a company or high profile organization, to public events.

Delegates: The main term used to describe people who attend conferences, seminars, workshops and similar events.

Event co-ordinator: The individual who manages an event on behalf of a client.

Event organizer: The individual, or organization, who promotes and manages an event.

Guaranteed number: The minimum number of guests at an event.

Logistics: The discipline of planning and organizing the flow of goods, equipment and people to their point of use.

Participant: A person attending an event who is actively taking part in it, or in some activity related to it.

Public Event: An event attended by members of the general public.

Seminar: Describes small gatherings similar to the breakout sessions, where a group will discuss an issue.

Set-up time: The time needed to arrange the necessary facilities for the event.

VIP: Very Important Person.

Workshop: A small gathering of people to discuss a specific topic or solve a particular problem.

Bibliography

Shenson, Howard. How To Develop & Promote Successful Seminars and Workshops: The Definitive Guide to Creating and Marketing Seminars, Workshops, Classes and Conferences. John Wiley & Sons, 1990

Laois County Enterprise Board, Publications, 20 July 2011, http://www.laoisenterprise.com/page.asp?cid=1126